EARLY
Rhythms

"I'm immediately struck by the sense of nature and the elemental always present in her words. The importance of water and air and fire. At the same time, there's a softness and an opening, a permeability to the world and her ever-present sense that this life is a balance between wanting and allowing. In truth, these feel not so much poems as an ongoing conversation between selves that are remembering more clearly as each moment unfolds. Or the voice of a friend lying in grass beside us in the soft night, wandering together in an endless sea of stars. As she writes so beautifully: Time is fast and fleeting. Nothing is certain. Don't let go of things that are rare and beautiful and true."

—BRIAN ANDREAS, artist, author at
A Hundred Ways North and *Storypeople*

"Rhythms and Roads is a moving collection of transmissions & messages from the universe, & mostly, a moving remembering for our very own hearts."

—BRYONIE WISE, author of *Heart Roar:*
A Book of Tiny Prayers

"An enthusiastic stream of wild beauty and magic, Victoria's poetry and prose creates footprints on an epic adventure of soul. I'm nourished and inspired daily, by Victoria's artistry, her visions and child-like love for Life. Her wise expression is the road trip of this lifetime, leading us all back to our own dreaming, seeking hearts."

—TANYA MARKUL, creator of *ThugUnicorn.com*, *WakingWild.com* and *TheUrbanHowl.com*

"Living a creative life can be both magical and maddening. It requires a kind of curiosity and vulnerability not for the faint of heart. Through her elegant and eloquent way of weaving words together on the page, Victoria shows us that strength can be both soft and subtle, and that life rewards us in unexpected ways when we dare to live so boldly that we are broken open. These are words I can live by."

—ALISA BARRY, artist, author & entrepreneur at *Alisabarry.com*

"If you want to feel your feelings, then go read anything written by Victoria Erickson. She is a lighthouse whose words ignite and touch the soul like nothing else I have ever

read or experienced before." Rhythms and
Roads is another brilliant book that inspires
us to live from a place of authenticity and
connection."

—ELISE MUSELES, founder of Kale & Chocolate
and author of *Whole Food Energy*

"Victoria Erickson is an alchemist of the
human spirit. Her words are the kind we
reach for to make sense of our messy hearts
and labyrinth minds. She gives voice to the
feelings you can taste but cannot name. The
things you choke on when the night is never-
ending. Bring her your pain and she will
give you a song."

—ERIN MERELLI, founder at *Voyage of the Soul*

"I slip into Victoria's words and swiftly
I'm able to feel differently. There's a soft
mirror-soul. Her words, enchanting, engaging,
and enriching are a dreaming reflection
of endless, hopeful and poignant. How is it
possible to string the right sequence together
and create her magic? It just is. I only want
more."

—CAROLYN RIKER, author of *Blue Clouds*

"The rush of her words pierces directly to my soul. Victoria has (once again) captured the essence of her spirit, of our deepest thoughts and energies, and of the collective voice. As an old-soul poet, her wisdom and her inspiration are the daily dose we all need. Rhythms and Roads is a bedside book, for as the moment you open your eyes in the morning, or say goodnight to the moon and stars, Victoria's words will be right there with you."

—GERRY ELLEN, author of *Ripple Effects* and *A Big Piece of Driftwood*

"Eye-opening, mind-opening, and heart-opening, Rhythms & Roads is full of beautiful reminders, insights, and hope. Victoria Erickson weaves observations of her outer and inner worlds with a grounded reality that also inspires. She presents not just poetry, but supportive teachings that engage the senses as well as the mind. Her words have both the power and the softness to move you."

—REBECCA CLIO GOULD, author of *The Multi-Orgasmic Diet*

Rhythms and Roads

Victoria Erickson

ENREALMENT PRESS
TORONTO, CANADA

Published by Enrealment Press
PO Box 64
Acton, Ontario
Canada L7J 2M2

Cover photo by Thomas Zsebok/Shutterstock
Cover and Book Design by Susan Frybort and go-word.com
Printed in the USA

Library and Archives Canada Cataloguing in
Publication

 Erickson, Victoria, author
        Rhythms and roads / Victoria Erickson.

Poems.
ISBN 978-0-9947843-5-3 (paperback)

        I. Title.

PS3605.R535R49 2016   811'.6   C2016-904816-0

I dedicate this book to my teachers, my lessons, my amazing family, my supportive publisher, the ones I've loved, and the ones I've lost. I also dedicate this book to all the free spirits breathing the medicine of new rhythms and roads into an often stagnant world. The ones courageous enough to choose truth, and growth.

Rhythms and Roads

Victoria Erickson

There are thousands of worlds
in all of us.
Gorgeous, terrible,
wild, contradictory,
imaginative fascinating worlds.
To know someone deeply
is to know a universe
contained in skin.

We sped through the night
weightless without plans,
chasing moonlight across
miles and roads,
adulthood as many years away
as we wanted it.
We dreamed up ways
to make freedom real.

Sometimes someone isn't ready
to see the bright side.
Sometimes they need to sit
with the shadow first.
So be a friend and sit with them.
Make the darkness beautiful.

You cannot seek water
from the one
who drained your seas,
and you cannot build
a home for your worth
inside of another being.
The medicine is when
you return to yourself
where you will remember
your strength,
reclaim your own rhythm,
and write your new song.

Love like mammals
without shielding
or guarding.
Without planning
or worrying.
Just a full-blown run,
relentless and river-like,
and wild without war.
This is when
the earth moves.

The important, life altering things
hardly ever knock.
They pour and burn
and sweep in from somewhere
that feels like a sky.
Things like urgency.
A calling. Desire.
Turning points.
Things like love.

Saying 'no' is often
an opening to something wilder,
and worthier,
and truer.

It is not about
being loved, my love.
It is about radiating it
from the inside out.
Feeling the connection
between all that breathes,
and you.
Live alongside life.
This is how to exist beautifully.

When your senses are written
across your body,
continuously reaching for,
soaking in,
and gathering every detail
of your wide outer world,
you may be an artist.

To me, love isn't the opposite of hate.
It's the opposite of fear.
Maybe we can burn away fear
using love as the flame.
Maybe we can consciously hold that burn
any time fear attempts to return.
Maybe we can become
the very fire itself.

There will come a time
when you'll meet acceptance.
Your shoulders will soften,
the sky will stretch on,
and the night will hold a pulse
both electric and warm.
And the moon will feel familiar.

Solitude isn't loneliness.
Solitude is when
the entire serene universe
seems to surround
and hold you quietly.

I sometimes cannot
simply let things slide.
I'm an ocean, so I write.
And when you're made of water,
that part of the self evaporates
as soon as it's released.
I'll write about a situation
'til it's gone,
so a sea of betrayal
turns to nothing
but salt on sand.
Some of us don't let things slide,
as we don't have slide mechanisms.
Just drains.

On disappointment:
Don't immediately brush it off.
Feel it first,
then it will leave you quicker.
Here's the thing
about broken glass:
it needs to be acknowledged
and swept up
so you don't step on it later.

Artists feel what they're carrying
and feel it vividly.
In order to make their art pulse,
they must find their edges
and soften there.
Art (like love)
was never about safety.
To love an artist
is to fall into a sea
of deep, soulful,
courageous, wild living.

Part of reclaiming your power
is recognizing that the individual
you'd handed it over to
was never worthy or deserving
of it anyway.

You should probably not
shut down and lock away
the more terrified,
messy parts of yourself.

Expectation breeds exasperation,
as it's simply an illusive form of control
by attempting to grip the reins
that aren't ours to hold.
Breathe. Release.
Let go.
Allow your life naturally,
quietly unfold.

Decisions are never made
when we most want to make them.
I think over time,
we simply tumble
into what we've been pulled toward.
Our feet try and brake.
Our arms stretch to block the fall.
The ground awaits.
The sky holds its breath.
The shift then arrives to claim us,
while naming the path
we hadn't seen.

If you're stuck on an idea,
a memory, or decision,
go do something
that drowns the thinking
such as anything that creates
movement, fluidity, and flow.
Your body forever wants to be
ignited and replenished in this way.
Because we are made
and born of water.

They ask what inspires you.
When a voice breaks
against your shoulder.
When you're expected to ask,
plead, or beg.
When they tell you
they don't believe you.
The scent of smoke or leather
drifting across this air.
The way they shrugged
in that second of time
you'll soon long to forget,
yet will stretch across years to come.
Too much or not enough,
or the taste of syrup,
or curve of a hip,
or one hundred unseen doors.
The sound of a train
ripping through silence,
swallowing all unknowns.
Rooftops and beliefs
and those once quieted words.
Words that belonged
between you and them.
Words that never landed.
Words that needed a home.

To me, 'going gently' means
that you're the alchemist
of your own rhythm and peace.
You and you alone can mold it,
the way a bird owns
the piece of sky
it's been flying toward.

Trade in electricity
for wildfires
and maybes
for affirmative answers.
Shed the unnecessary.
Find the solid center.
Go. Stand strong
on that gentle ledge.
Use your fingers to trace
the horizon.
It is vast but you are fierce.
Know you can go beyond it.

There are some days you wish
you could live out 10,000 more times.
It's almost as though all the other days
seemed to rise and fall and prepare
and propel you toward these certain ones,
holding you like a dream you've only now
remembered.
The magic ones
you quietly know will change everything.
They shift the view.
They open the channel.
They offer the light.

Who said sunsets were enough?
And who said they weren't?
I know things can't be solved
or built by gazing into flames,
but you can still grip those hues
and hold them as the earth moves,
and think it to be true.

How do you find your power?
You catch glimpses.
You begin to trust them.
Then the more you trust them,
the more the picture unfolds.
The more the picture unfolds,
the larger it grows.
It all begins with
trusting beginnings.

Creative writing is writing
from the body and senses.
Not from the mind.
The body continuously
goes through natural cycles,
and we must trust them.
It's an ongoing process
of becoming and growth,
and death over and over.
The creative process
echoes nature.

One winter seems to last for years
in places like this.
Grey sky touching grey ground
Days turn to nights
and nights turn to days
until the landscape itself
becomes neutrally indifferent.
How restless it is to remain awake
as the earth sleeps below us.
How easy it is to turn into ourselves
and think too hard for too long
until we too, become indifferent.
I refuse to become indifferent.

The deeper the burn,
the truer the fire.
Fire is always worthy of watching.
Of knowing. Of having.
To feel the life in it seize on
and spark the life within you.

I'll always want to drive with you.
I'll always want to trace
all the corners of the world
with my own bare hands.
We'll whirl by the exits like flight.
Like wind.
Two birds collecting stories.
Breaking all cages.
Chasing our whims.

Transformation itself
isn't a joy.
The joy is in
the freedom
that arrives
just past
the threshold.
It rushes through.
Released like rain.

Are you tired of
everything confusing?
Sometimes the sea
can't separate
from the rain
and the pleasure can't tell itself
from the pain
and the time has washed over us
the way it weighs
on human shoulders.
The way it treads on
yet falls exactly the same.
There are miles and miles
of roads ahead.
The way to heal
is to pick a route.
To walk the path.
To make that choice.
To finally decide.
Because we cannot remain
stuck as we are
in this status quo,
forever caught
and kept inside
of this dark, indecisive,
splitting divide.

Of course at first it was thrilling.
Before reality and soot
and the way time turns over
as this earth continued to spin. To move.
You wish you could pause it all,
throw yourself across the many months
that've stretched like wide golden fields.
Remember the beginning.
Develop the mindset.
Recall the hunger.
Use the correct tools.
But instead, you must go on.
You must keep walking.
There's light in the letting go.

Time is fast and fleeting.
Nothing is certain.
Don't let go of things
that are rare and beautiful and true.

Sometimes we must force ourselves
to drop every story,
decision, motivation, expectation
or tiny pain that's ever gripped us
prior to this moment.
Forget the things
that happened then.
You're here now.
And the Now desires you.
In a way you don't yet realize.

It doesn't always have to be so much work.
You can't spend all of your days
always fighting against the tides,
chained to the doors
you cannot seem to break,
like a servant to those clocks
as you race against the time.
Stop treading and swimming so hard.
It's okay sometimes to float.
To simply trust the water.

We spend too much time in our heads.
Analyzing. Wondering.
Asking. Planning. Stop.
Come back to here, now.
Where I am,
it's mid afternoon
in late summer.
The sunlight is flooding
the grass and ground.
It feels still.
And all is well.

You tried to seek beauty
without them in the world,
hauling your heart
across the valleys and plains,
your eyes thirsty
for those flowers.
It took years
before spring returned.

Sometimes the easiest way
to find out who you are
is to be around those
where you don't have to be
anything at all.
Except you. As you are.
Here. Now.

In every heartache
or disappointment,
or difficulty,
beauty rushes in.

The night has as many answers
as it has questions,
as many conclusions
as it has longings,
and as it drenches us in darkness,
it sheds all we've carried to light.
We crawl back to the dreams
that have slipped through our days.
The body moves through afternoons.
The soul breathes through our nights.

This isn't always a world for hearts.
Sometimes the heart needs convincing
to leave the quiet rooms of soft safety.
Its thirst has a real taste,
and we cannot access the truth of a heart
without first opening
the windows and doors to quench it.
You should know today (not someday)
that you're allowed this,
and deserve it.
It is later than we think.

Be less interested
in defining yourself
as one thing
and more interested
in your glorious complexities.

Friends. Lovers. Co-workers.
How do we know they're good for us?
Forget bells and whistles
and one thousand other distractions.
Ask yourself:
can you simply be beside them?

When we grow tired of fields
we'll take to the western deserts,
the barren ground,
the golden dunes,
the wild skies.
I want to know
the lands that call to you in dreams.
The views that pull and haunt
and want you in the night.
And we will go.

Some people don't like lists.
I recommend filling pages with them.
Maybe I'll begin to share mine.
Lists to turn thoughts into letters.
Lists to recycle the old.
Lists to take tired, faded things
and make them burn again.
To write them alive.
Turn them into gold.

Remember that desire
is an important energy.
It's strong enough to carry us
through what we must burn to
actually reach what's been calling.

Storms make the earth honest.
They rattle the edges
and tear it to shreds
before gifting the calm again.
Your own hardships and storms
do the same to you.
They rinse you clean.
They paint new colors.
They deepen your understanding.
They give you new language.
A certain sweet serenity
not previously known.

Are you not ready?
Or are you scared?
There is a difference.
A space between the two.
Sometimes every moment
is the right moment
because you simply
have to do it.

I don't own a TV.
I prefer music that takes me.
Words upon words.
Worlds that work and weave
through my imagination
the way books
and illustrations would,
as a child.
This is how we consciously
create the soundtracks
to our lives.

If you want to expect things,
only expect them from yourself.
Don't take the reins
of anything or anyone else.
This is how to remain on the horse.
By only riding your own.

I just wanted to speak from experience
that you should do
the absolutely insane crazy thing,
the thing that pulls you in the night,
defying sense and logic and plans
because I decided to take that route
and I struggled.
But I remained tied to the words
like a cord that couldn't break
because I believed that something
that felt so impossibly,
uncomfortably strong
just couldn't be wrong.
You need to trust your body.
It already knows the way.

I'm not sure what the world
would be like without dogs.
Dogs bring you back to what's true
when people are running about performing
with masks and lines all over the stage.

So at what point do you
become really tired of yourself
and all the ways you shut down
what you kind of
(yet won't admit it
but it's so very intriguing
so maybe you do actually want it) desire?
It's just voltage. Sonic boom.
No roads back. An opening.
And everything is (just there) waiting for you.

It all comes back to energy.
And we use far too much energy
thinking and deciding.
Sometimes it's really as simple
as do or do not,
and taking freeing,
liberating action
in one of those
two directions.

Sometimes you don't feel
the burning rush of words.
Sometimes the fire's softer (like water),
the way you occasionally need it.
Sometimes important realizations
come to us gently.

We all have a bit of everyone else in us,
and this is just part of our drive to read
and watch and understand.
Because seeing ourselves in them
reminds us again and again
that we aren't an island of confinement
within our own brains- we're instead part
of this wide,
pulsing galaxy called the collective,
and as different as we are,
we're also very, very similar.
So remember you are never, never alone.
You are actually "we."
Let's continually hold each other up,
calmly.

These crazy things happen FOR you,
not to you.
For you to be bigger,
to be stronger,
to be better.
And for you to be
far wiser.

Dear artist, what happens to you
is less visible, less obvious,
and more underground.
You see things
and keep silent about them.
You listen. You note.
You understand.
And you remember.
Then you tell secret things
to your piano or page or paintbrush
until the feeling and fire and flow
leave your flesh.
It's messy and gorgeous,
and dangerously raw.
This is why they refer
to art as love.

Things are terrible and amazing
and confusing
and busy and beautiful and awe inspiring
and terrible again and then there are
these days that are so quiet outside
you can almost hear an acorn fall.
Because sometimes the world closes,
and the moon swells, and time slows,
and suddenly you'll remember
for just a day to drop all else,
and to choose (and remember) love.

Remember that you are
more than just blood and breath.
You are one thousand stories of before.
One thousand stories of potential.
One thousand stories you've yet to see
and know and feel and breathe.
There's more to come.
And it's something beautiful.

Greetings and goodbyes: a love story.
When we say, "good morning"
or "goodnight"
to our friends or children
or anyone we love,
we are wrapping that person in light
for awhile,
until the day turns over the way days do,
until we meet again in time.
These words hold intention
and vibration,
setting forth a ritual
that always chooses the side of love,
churning the stories
of the previous hours
into something that remains well
despite any situation that arose
within our sight.
Never underestimate the power
of "good morning" and "goodnight."

If you have lived
and experienced,
then tell it.
Perhaps you've held in
those stories too long,
like plants stuck underground,
knowing the air is up here.
Stems reaching for the light.
Craving the sky.
Sensing and desiring the sound.
There's freedom in the telling.

You'll know when it's time to heal.
And you will always travel inwardly,
among your deep grooves and rivers,
returning with full hands,
ready to release light
into your external aching world.

I'm a sky gazer because
it takes the glass
and spills the liquid
and feeds me all of it, always.
Gaze up instead of across,
and your skies
will be your seas,
revealing everything
you've never known about life,
presence, and loss.

Be sure to rise into love with yourself.
Because everything you need
is already alive within you.
Anything else that comes
is just a catalyst that calls it.

I'll remind you ten thousand times
as life has the ability
to break you in ten thousand ways
and yet you still keep
rinsing and rising
and reclaiming
the beautiful being you are,
have been, and always will be.
Feel your life while you're in it
every passing day because,
would you really ever want it
any other way?

I'm now drained by the burden
of longing.
The disappointments.
The wondering when's.
We must draw our own horses.
Breathe them into being.
And never hand the reins
to anyone else, again.

I hope you're as smitten
with the moon as I am.
The silence and serenity
and wild mystery
it demonstrates all at once.
We don't always
have to talk or explain
or do to be radiant.
There is power
in the subtleties.

We're made of layers
and mysteries and oceans.
Starlight and darkness
and history and bone.
The human psyche is fascinatingly
complex.
It can take a lifetime
to know someone deeply.
We send radar, we learn slowly,
we recognize what's buried in us
may be buried in them.
We learn over time
what does and what doesn't
feel like home.

You looked for them
but the streets were empty,
all sidewalks covered in shadows.
In rain.
How dark the buildings get
once these storms
grip the ground.
Once these mistakes
have been
written, and made.
You would've stood
in the doorway
alongside this water,
and thunder,
and pale moon,
and midnight sound.
And held them
like the earth moves.

And sometimes it's all enough.
Exactly where we are
in every direction.
Trust that beyond the doors
that aren't opening
or the signs that aren't showing
that here and now,
this is exactly
and mysteriously enough.

The colors you're choosing
are settling into the mosaic of you.
You stare into it seeing memory.
Choices. Experience.
It stares into you, seeing itself.
Color. Shadows.
Splashes. Light.
Space. Potential.

A world without heart
is a world without a capacity to heal,
to create, to connect and to listen.
Underneath the veneer of our lives
exists the often times
unknowingly dull ache
of both predictability and drain.
The heart is where the shift happens.
It's raw, it's vital and it's necessary.

Instant illumination rarely happens.
Your tiny revelations
will seep in stitch by stitch.
Rest the reaching.

Small talk is fun sometimes.
And sometimes we don't always
want to talk of things
that may feel hard or hurt.
But I'm not much of a pretender.
The real feeds me.
If I know you,
I want both your joy and pain.
Whatever is real in that moment.
Let's not be pretenders.

I've learned that seeking
is sometimes simply
touching the land that calls you.
Returning to places that feed you.
Knowing the homes where you're carried
and full of life.
The ground that
breathes your truths.
We all have them.
We all know them.

Whenever in doubt,
come back to your belly.
Even if you don't want to hear
what it's telling you.
Even if this choice
right here in your core
is the most inconvenient, difficult,
stress inducing,
bite-the-bullet choice,
it won't be going away.
Emotions are fleeting.
Gut feelings are not.
You don't have to act
on anything right now.
But you will.

In order to sort out the chaos,
complications and confusions,
we must come back to
the simplest thing we do know.
What feels like nourishment?
Begin with that.

Today is the first day of forever.
So what will you do?
How could you open enough
to heal your wounds,
and let the surge of the world come
pouring through?

When others disappoint you:
Empty out. Cry. Exercise.
Shatter the image
of who you imagined or thought
they were, or "that" was.
Embrace what is Now.
Remember yourself.
Rinse out the old.
Rise above.

Poetry is the pulse inside the depth.
It's the writing genre
that wastes no time
making the magic visible.
If I had to choose one thing
to read for the rest of my days,
give me poetry as to me,
it's the sweetest, most underground,
and fiercest of all writing genres.

Bring me your dark—
split open yourself
and show me the glass;
I'll sweep through you like sun
until there's nothing left
but blazing brilliance.

Resistance only causes
disturbance and stagnancy.
Rivers must flow freely
To remain fresh
and beautiful.
To resist
is to cloud the water
with brown muck and mud.
To flow is to clearly reflect
a sky full of sunlight
and galaxy of stars.
The sweet spot
exists within the flow
and the flow
is only found in
the surrender.

Creativity is
your pressure valve
and energy
management system.
It saves your body
from carrying everything
you've lived, are living,
and dream of living.

The worst possible thing
in the world can happen
and the morning will come.
The sun will rise
same as it ever has.
You'll gaze out the window.
You'll stir your tea.
All is well.
And will be.

There's a turning point
where you have to jump
into something else.
Then there's an uncomfortable
transition.
But here's the thing about jumps:
you regain the energy
for the new thing
that the old thing
once consumed.

Darling, stand
tall inside the
discomfort of change.
Let it wash over you.
Drink the water.
Eat the salt.
Tell your body
it's better than fine.
You are being
cleansed and renewed
and you'll love
the new horizon.
But for now,
you must trust
the moods
of waves.

On creating:
don't be seeking or searching
for interesting things.
That's not how you do it.
Do it because it haunts
or asks or desires
or calls and you need to
sink your lungs and heart
and core and arms
straight in
until it seeps out
on to pages, instruments
or canvases.
This is where
the pulse lives.

You'll eventually wonder how things
would've turned out differently
if only you'd written it.
Told it. Said it. Did it.
Took forward action,
wrapped it around you
and owned it.
Don't bank on someday.
Someday is only
and always now.
And now.

Transformation isn't sweet and bright.
It's a dark and murky, painful pushing.
An unraveling of the untruths
you've carried in your body.
A practice in facing
your own created demons.
A complete uprooting
before becoming.

Love like the city
is burning.
Like the bright green
of June.
Like the sea might
run out of salt.
Like the sky loves
the ground,
quenching it with
heat and moonlight
and rain.
But never leave
and lose yourself
to love someone else.

This isn't where the book ends, love.
It's just where the chapter
turns into another.
A turning page
is also a turning point.
Inked progression.
Let this pen move freely.

A gypsy soul isn't lost and looking.
A gypsy soul is one who loves movement
and finding the pulse in nature
and flight as a metaphor.
One who thinks
everything is music.
One who knows and holds
an inward and therefore
outwardly contagious
kind of freedom.

What if rather than falling
for the object of your desire,
you fell for your desire itself?
The way your brain and blood
create burns as brilliantly bold as that.
How your flare can move and melt
the heaviest of mountains
blocking that wanted path.
We create our own arrows.
We're moved by what
we've made ourselves.

We were in the country somewhere.
Watermelon and grassy fields
under the bluest of skies,
stretched for miles and miles
as wide as they stood high.
We caught the slightest hint of smoke-
perhaps a bonfire from faraway
or maybe us and our space itself,
between the sun, the heat,
and the spark between you and I,
filled with serenity and ground
and wild, grinning eyes.
I'm often held and rocked
by the memory of fire and summer
and us in the countryside.
Because we remember moments.
Moments are what count.
Not the answers.
Not the events.
Not the destinations.
Not the questions.
Not the passage of time.

When we grow tired of fields
we'll take to the western deserts,
the barren ground,
the golden dunes, the wild skies.
I want to know the lands
that call to you in dreams.
The views that pull and haunt
and want you in the night.
And we will go.

I want to retrain
the memories in your heart.
I want to bathe them in light
so they finally release the ice
they have gathered
from slamming and pressing
against all that's been
hard, and sharp.

You've landed now,
with legs full of the earth
and hair full of the rain
that cleansed and renewed
and gave you yourself again.
You're now building your world
with wiser hands.
Worship the storm that dropped you here.
It gave you new language.

Someone told me once
about the consequence of time.
How something I maybe
never truly wanted
to unclasp
slowly drifts away
from this hand
and space beneath
these ribs
that I myself
made the choice
to reclaim.
To take back.
Until the tides
finally come
and wash
that something away,
now scattered like sand
across all that has
swallowed the memory
I once could not shake.

They never taught us
about edges.
How magical.
How difficult.
How dangerous.
How necessary.
They give us vision.
Motivation.
New oxygen.
Breath.
They clarify.

If a year was tucked
inside of a clock,
then autumn
would be
the magic hour.

Poems are both
the doing and undoing.
Electric prayers and sonnets.
Hope deeper than blood and bone.
Wounds you can place your hand on.

The most crucial wars
are the ones
within ourselves.

Don't think about the river and flow.
Feel the river and flow.
This is how you move
and merge weightlessly
with water.

Don't reach for
the answers at this time.
They'll eventually arrive
and when they do,
they'll be soft.
Much like an old friend
stepping back into our lives
as though they'd never actually
been gone at all.

You can carry a dream
as you'd carry a bouquet,
tucked inside your ribcage.
Until eventually the buds
will bend against skin,
struggling to breathe,
choking and desperate
to climb upward,
needing to burst
from the ache
to break free.
Break.
Don't be afraid.
Dreams are birthed by
wild hearts
and wild hearts
are as strong
as branches are
determined,
and roots run
strong and deep.

If only nights could be extended
without losing sleep
for clarity and creative purposes,
while somehow allowing us
to bottle those conclusions
and sprinkle them throughout
our afternoons
as a reminder of what comes to light
in between the moon and you.

When you're an ocean,
you cannot break yourself
by bending into the pond
someone else has limited you to.

Forget what's safe or shallow.
Go after bone deep,
full-blooded adventure
with those who can meet you
where your flame is here
and elsewhere, body and mind.
Become a force of life by knowing
what you want and won't accept.
Be sure to guard your time.

For those who are tied to the stars,
your calm is not enough.
They insist on knowing your ideals
and edges,
diving into the light of this feeling,
tracing your shadows with knowing hands,
expanding your future wider
with open palms over time.
But be careful.
If you try to tame and temper love,
maneuvering the natural course
of these tides,
you might be left swimming
in murky, dark waters
with fading stars still in your eyes,
recalling the way it had felt
in the sky.

I'd like to meet you in a place
neither of us has been
with sunlight and white buildings
and blue seas and golden hills.
I'd like to hike and stretch
and swim and then
find music so good
it melts our shoulders,
ears and eyes.
I'd like to share vibrant food
and care for you,
be calm with you,
learn your rhythms,
your mannerisms,
dive into your mind.
I'd like to know you,
yet not worry about knowing you,
and realize that all we have is now,
and that in the now,
there's no such thing as time.

Today I'm going to fall in love
with the way I belong to myself,
regardless of any situation,
or circumstance,
or commitment,
or outside happening.
I'm going to fall in love
with the way
I refuse to settle for less
than vibrant aliveness,
less than what feeds
and fuels this energy wildly.
Fully. Infinitely. Freely.
Because I'll allow nothing
on the outside
to detract from,
limit, lessen,
or shrink this.
Or me.

Time is momentum which means
it keeps moving but the beautiful
(and sometimes problematic) thing
about certain moments is that although
they have long since passed,
they never quite lose their momentum.
They sometimes circle around
and around and again
and again to the surface.
Twenty years may have slipped by
and the image is still developing.
Still existing.

Living in the moment isn't just about
having a grand old time
and getting swept up
into your current activity.
It's also about asking yourself
what's tangible and true here and now.
Let go of the old story
and come back
to what is current.

When you're deeply sensitive,
love is ecstasy.
Music is godlike.
Heartache is a wide, somatic wound.
Visual natural beauty is
jewel-drenched, wild bliss.
Tension and conflict are
muscle tightening and toxic,
straight down to the cells.
So how do you hold it all?
You rinse, recenter,
and remain clear.
You recycle your sensitivity
by propelling yourself and others
to create waves of change
in a super-starving world.
You harness what is the best,
and breathe out the excess,
allowing nothing disruptive or
harmful to stand in your way.

The night lovers
tend to be the seekers,
the dreamers, the writers,
the lovers,
and the progressive thinkers.
Things tend to make more sense
inside the quieter hours.

I've always been drawn to rocks.
All forms of them:
mountains, caves, canyons, cliffs.
They are perfectly wild, ancient art,
familiar and serene,
and the closest we get
to the heart and belly of the world.

I believe in longing.
In sitting in it, in feeling it,
in breathing in it.
Longing reminds us
that we are alive,
and that being alive
is to know that we are built for feeling.
Don't be a stranger to your body
while you're in it.

Remain soft.
Softness is weightlessness.
Softness is golden.
Softness is freedom.

Relationships are our clearest, most
present mirrors.
Choose the ones that strengthen you,
not the ones that weaken.
Because there's someone out there,
someone that will want all that you are
in this gorgeously massive universe.
A mirror that is simple, and steady.

Scent is our greatest,
most potent form
of time travel,
like an arrow.
It tears through layers.
It finds the center.

Betrayal can reveal itself
in numerous ways.
And when it does,
it rips you open.
It gives you to the ground.
It carves new ways of wanting.
It grips and it burns
and later becomes your gift.

How to be weightless:
Set fire to the clutter.
Infuse boundaries.
Allow music to linger long after
it's been felt.
Soften. Rip old strings.
Find sanctuaries.
Touch thresholds.
Soak in water.
Know your rhythms.
Read the words.
Become the very poem itself.

Obstacles are merely tests to see
how badly you want it.
To find how much heat
and grit you hold.
The universe bows
to who you believe
yourself to be.

The medicine you seek
lives within your deepest,
shadowed, truest parts.
Resist the relentless urge
to search for it in places,
substances, experiences,
or other burning,
bleeding, breathing hearts.
You are your own drug.

To love is to
hold me when I am raining.
To breathe me when I am burning.
To release me when I am running.

Wonder is one of the wildest elements
and qualities on the massive scale
of human experience.
Just a pinch of it stops time.
The world halts.
The eyes fill.
You become, for a small time,
everything you truly are.

Control was never yours.
Loosen the grip and slowly
open each palm.
Let it go.
Breathe the good things
into being.
Let these feed
and teach you.
Because they will.

On artists:
They'll probably know you
deeper than you know yourself,
calling you to the root of your shape.
The tides will feel stronger
and time will no longer seem linear.
You'll be blinded and taken by light.
You'll learn of hidden doors
in the dark.

Release the need to know
why that thing happened.
Because you know what?
It doesn't matter.
What matters is reclaiming the fire
it'll take to rebuild your energy again.
And what matters is rediscovering
the ridiculous amount of beauty right here,
and right now straight into the pulsing,
tangible, gloriously sweet center
of this and only this
present moment.
What matters is now.
Not then.

It doesn't have to be so difficult and gossipy
and hyper competitive and false.
If only everyone would see that
kids, plants, and dogs know everything.
That trivial things shouldn't become monsters.
That stress in itself solves nothing.
That we are all confused
and yet so cosmic
and bloody brilliant.
Oh and the carried inner conflicts
and work it takes to win them
are worth the fight one thousand times over,
and the thing blocking the path
is also the path.
And that nothing is unrelated.
Everything is interrelated and intertwined
like stitches across a giant,
breathing quilt of color and consciousness.
And that being alive is awesome.
That is all.

I'd like to talk to people deeply.
I'd like to drive the southwest
and sleep under dying stars
and breathe all the things
my lungs have ached to know and do.
I want to have conversations
with the ancient, wild light
that is the moon.
She'll tell me about mystery,
and tides, and night.
And I'll tell her about you.

Hearts are not flowery.
They're wild electric power centers.
And like poetry,
romance isn't
light surface sweetness.
It is the dark and deep
well of the cup.

Never apologize for the way
you choose to heal.
Drain your waters of the muck.
Clear out the garbage.
Sternly draw the boundary.
Protect your precious ocean.

Just because you are strong
doesn't mean you are not a force.
Honey and wildfire are both
the color gold.

The music, images, and words
you soak in run through you.
They flow somewhere between
memory and dream,
ultimately becoming your river
of influence, illumination,
and inspiration.

Every morning you rise,
I want you to remember this:
there are amazing things to be a part of
and fight for and feel
because the world will unlock
hundreds of doors
when you give this day
all the courage, love,
and intensity you can.

There are no restrictions
on the gorgeous resurrection
and revolution
that reveals itself
when settling into
your own imperfect self and skin.
And there is no shame
in admitting that this
hasn't always been the place
you've held in the highest regard,
but you are showing up now.
And you are trying.

I can't get enough
of wandering.
Or the earth.
Some of us carry
an inherent need to explore.
Textures. Fragrances.
Sounds. Air.
Shadows. Movement.
Patterns. Light.

You don't write
to build worlds.
You write to spill them
like liquid
across a page.
The worlds that
already breathe
and unravel
and seek
and demand.

Wanderlust is an aching condition
that strikes unexpectedly
and refuses to
release its electric grip.
It never asks for permission.
It just knocks your doors down.

You know the people in your life
you don't have to dance
around the core with?
How there's no need for small talk,
just a straight sort of dive
into the center of things?
How you just consistently vibe
both playfully and seriously?
Hold onto those people.

Rather than worrying about
how to keep 'their' attention,
or appearing appealing,
or attempting to extract
a lake of validation
from a slow-drip faucet,
maybe simply
come back to yourself.

Think about the crystals in sand.
The breath in the trees.
How the grip always softens.
How the body holds the light.
Redirect your energy
to things that quench.
Things that awaken.
Things that uplift.
Things that feed.
Come back to your heart and blood.
Their rhythm. Their circle.
Their consistency. Their heat.
Now let your river of old patterns
fall out like moving water.
Through, below, and beneath.

Release your thoughts,
for they are merely storms
you have clung to.
Return to the shore
of your body.
Breathe the warm light
your lungs
had forgotten.

To be vulnerable
is to know lightness,
and flight.
How it feels to
break old barriers
and walls.
To be
unrestricted.
Free.

There is a massive difference
between fire and Hell.
Do not let a person guide you
down pathways of pain
and call it passion.

Stay soft.
For the sake of anyone
who cannot feel or swim
inside of their own skin,
caught between built barriers
now solid as stone.
Show them the depths of seas.
The language of water.

Carry hope as recklessly
as you'd like to.
It's a living, breathing thing
that seeks you like sun.
It can stretch as far
as you need it to.
Don't be afraid of horizons
and nights.
When hope falls
it always returns.

I always want to bottle
the scent of morning.
The mix of hope and arrival
and dew and energy.
If morning owned an element,
it would be air.
Air is equal parts
oxygen, daydreams
and possibility.

To be fed by wildness
is to desire nature
so deeply
you find bliss
everywhere.
Every day.
Every hour.
Waiting.
Reaching for you.

Sensitivity is the sword
that cuts through dullness,
the mundane,
and any disenchantment.
Continue to sharpen
and tune this.
Your body was made for feeling.
When you grow more sensitive
you're ultimately respecting
and bowing to your body.
And that is beautiful.

Confidence is silent and subtle.
Insecurities are loud and obvious.
The most powerful ones
do not need to announce
their own influence
or impress.
It runs too deep
to be a billboard.
It is embodied and sensed
because they simply are.
And do.

We are not physically or mentally
made for stagnancy.
We are always either growing or dying.
The only way to grow
is to continually challenge ourselves,
or swim through challenge,
even when we have waves of weakness.
When you can know,
admit, and name your weaknesses aloud,
you are no longer weak anymore.
You've then become the strong one.
Stagnancy is the rock that sinks us.
Choose growth and movement.
Know your own ocean, and own it.

Every time you write,
you remove another mask.
A layer upon a layer.
Another door to another room.
You reveal who you are to yourself.

When night falls,
peel off your sadness.
Give it to the galaxies.
Your organs will shine again by sunrise.
This is the language of fire.

Boundaries are not walls.
They're your beaches
others can bask on.
Not everyone should swim
your oceans.

Listen to your skin.
Walk the earth.
Think about summer.
Learn about love.
Remember you cannot fail
as all you can do is change.
And change is always
an adventure.
And adventure
Is always worthwhile.

You've got to fall in love
with the shadow.
Everyone has it.
You cannot deny it,
or run from it, or empty it,
or attempt to rise above it.
Swim in it instead. Listen to it.
Respect it. Bow to it.
Breathe it. Honor it.
Be fully fascinated by it.
Connected to it.
It can be harsh and demanding.
Sometimes cold and cruel.
But ultimately, it will teach you.
Guide you. Feed you.
Strengthen you. Mold you.
And it will free you.
Knowing your darkness
is what affords you the light.
We cannot feel the day
if we don't touch the night.
This is harmony.
This is wholeness.

I want to feel highways.
Wind. Exits. The night.
I want to drive until
there's nothing around us
but nothing.
Nothing.
Nothing.
I want to know you
like rivers
know the earth.
A love cutting
through stagnant ground.
Coursing cool water
quenching the veins
in us.
All that's gone stagnant,
and dry.

I want you to know one thing.
That in the heart and thick of it,
deep in the trenches of experience
and wonder and ancestry
and the darkest dark
and brightest light,
you are wildly, primally,
ravishingly magical.

Come. Find me here.
We'll be fire and dreams
pressing against the world.
Locking eyes with ancient stars.
Holding night inside
of our mouths.
Knowing bliss
has a real taste.

The minute you grip
onto something too tightly,
you become the addict,
and they become the dealer.
Breathe. Release your hold.
The natural state is gentle.
Freeing. An unchained flow.

Your name lives stifled
inside of my throat,
rising and falling
through aching lungs.
And I'll hold you there in silence,
never saying a thing,
forever wrapped in caution,
as this love holds its breath.
Glory to the ones
that follow their bodies.
All the ones who speak
from the beat in their chests.

Beauty appears
where there is an edge.
A type of courage.
A fearlessness against
the unknown.
Not where there
is perfection.

The older I get,
the more I recognize the value
of the full-blown YES.
Yes, you know you want this thing,
this opportunity, this jump,
this decision, this desire,
this town, or this person.
It could be slightly nerve wracking.
Or unsettling.
Maybe tiny traces of hesitation.
A few quiet doubts.
But these still don't change
the full YES factor.
Because anything less
than the realm of yes is a no.
And it's as difficult and simple
and as difficult
and as crushingly, blazingly,
beautifully, simple
(and freeing) as that.

I have so much respect,
appreciation and admiration
for all of you fascinating people
out there burning with intention,
creating, recreating, falling,
dusting and rising.
You really don't realize
how brilliantly beautiful you are,
breaking old beliefs
and grasping your bliss.
I realize it's ridiculously hard and messy
but you can do ridiculously hard and
messy things.
Are you shaken?
Good. Keep going.
You were shaken before
and here you are.
Still standing.
Doing this.
Shining and expanding
and gloriously undefined.

Reveal to me
a piece of yourself
one dusk after another.
Same as the moon does
with each of us.
A slow
and continuous,
subtle unveiling.

Becoming a servant
to your life's work
and passion
is a beautiful kind
of submission.
A great bowing
to the commands
of a mighty purpose
that's been lingering here,
with an outstretched hand,
quietly awaiting you.

Find me here.
Deep in the space
where belief undoes disbelief.
Rhythms and water.
Tides against land.
The remembering of this place.
The revealing and repair.
With eyes made of depths.
And trembling hands.
We'll find that light that was ours
and reclaim all that we'd lost
when we'd forgotten the ground.
We'll trace constellations
and build our castles
once again
with this sand.

About the Author

Victoria Erickson is a grounded idealist who's been writing the world awake since she was a child. Forever embodied and heart driven, she believes deeply in innate wildness, creativity, intuitive body intelligence, and in harnessing the power of sensitivity. A rising social media sensation, *Rhythms and Roads* follows the great success of her first book, *Edge of Wonder.* You can connect with Victoria's work on Facebook (Victoria Erickson, Writer), and Instagram (Victoriaericksonwriter).